MW01173546

25 Select Devotions from
Meeting God at Every Corner

by

Jamie Buckingham

Content compiled and edited by
Bruce and Michele Buckingham

Risky Living Ministries, Inc.

MGAEC Sampler
(a.k.a. Meeting God at Every Corner Sampler)
By Jamie Buckingham

Copyright © 2023 by Risky Living Ministries, Inc.

Unless otherwise noted, scripture quotes are taken from THE HOLY BIBLE, NEW INTERNATIONAL VERSION®, NIV® Copyright © 1973, 1978, by Biblica, Inc.® Used by permission. All rights reserved worldwide.

King James Version scripture references indicated by KJV.

Meeting God at Every Corner Sampler is produced by:

Risky Living Ministries, Inc.
3901 Hield Road NW
Palm Bay, FL 32907

www.RiskyLivingMinistries.com

Risky Living Ministries, Inc., is dedicated to preserving the teachings and life works of Jamie Buckingham.

ISBN: 9798373998888

Cover design by Kent Jensen (knail.com)

"A PRICELESS RESOURCE."
— BILL JOHNSON

365 DAILY DEVOTIONS FOR SPIRIT-LED LIVING

MEETING GOD AT EVERY CORNER

DEVOTIONAL

JAMIE BUCKINGHAM

COMPILED AND EDITED BY
BRUCE AND MICHELE BUCKINGHAM

GOD IS READY
AND WAITING TO MEET YOU

Meeting God at Every Corner is an exciting new 365-day daily devotional based entirely on the teachings of Jamie Buckingham, one of the best-known and best-loved Christian leaders of his time. Jamie was known for his unique ability to teach God's Word with grace, insight, transparency, and humor. Always relatable and accessible, Jamie sought to be Spirit-led in everything he said and did—and to encourage his fellow believers to do the same.

A decade in the making, this 365-day devotional is the compilation and capstone of Jamie's teachings, adapted from sermons recorded over a 22-year period. Each devotion is written to give you a fresh glimpse into the multi-faceted heart of God and to challenge and inspire you to be led by His Spirit.

Jamie's teaching is as relevant today as ever—and maybe more so, given the unique hour in which we live. Allow him to take you on this year-long, Spirit-led, Spirit-filled journey. Deepen your understanding of what it means to live each day as Jamie did, knowing that God is always there, ready and waiting to meet you at every corner.

Meeting God at Every Corner presents us with 365 opportunities to encounter God's heart, continuously reestablishing our identity as children of God. I can't imagine a better investment of our time.

—BILL JOHNSON, author of *Open Heavens* and *Mornings and Evenings in His Presence*,
Bethel Church, Redding, CA

Jamie touched multitudes of people, both those in the body of Christ and those not. He touched everyone, even children, with his uncommon sermons, his stories, his reminiscings—with his totally honest and unaffected approach.

—ORAL ROBERTS, hasling evangelist, founder of Oral Roberts University, Tulsa, OK

JAMIE BUCKINGHAM was an internationally recognized pastor, author, and leader in the Charismatic Movement from the early 1970s to his death in 1992. He wrote numerous books for Kathryn Kuhlman, Corrie ten Boom, Pat Robertson, and many others. His book *Run Baby Run* with Nicky Cruz became an international bestseller. His award-winning magazine columns and bestselling books, including *Risky Living*, *Where Eagles Soar*, and *A Way Through the Wilderness*, cemented his reputation as a transparent, approachable leader, an insightful Bible teacher, and a master storyteller. For more resources by Jamie Buckingham, please visit: WWW.JAMIEBUCKINGHAMMINISTRIES.COM

BRIDGE LOGOS

BRIDGELOGOS.COM

RELIGION | CHRISTIAN LIVING | DEVOTIONAL

ISBN 978-1-61036-272-6

9 781610 362726

FOREWORD

In this little book is a small sampling of the full
devotional experience that is awaiting you in *Meeting
God at Every Corner: 365 Daily Devotions for Spirit-
Led Living* by Jamie Buckingham. Each of the 365
devotions in *Meeting God*—25 of which are included
here—is taken directly from the sermons of Jamie
Buckingham preached over a 22-year period, from
December 1969 through and including his very last
sermon in January 1992.

Jamie was well-known as a writer, magazine columnist,
and author of over 40 books, including some he wrote
for other key leaders of his day, such as Corrie ten
Boom, Kathryn Kuhlman, and Pat Robertson. But first
and foremost, Jamie was a pastor at the church he started
from modest beginnings, the Tabernacle Church of
Melbourne, Florida, which grew to become the largest
congregation in the region. Besides preaching at "The
Tab," Jamie was a popular conference speaker, teaching
in numerous churches and at various Christian venues
around the world. It is from these spoken teachings—at
his own church and in other pulpits—that the 365
devotions in *Meeting God at Every Corner* are drawn.

The writing and compiling of *Meeting God* was the
vision of Jamie's eldest son, Bruce. Feeling prompted by
God to share Jamie's timeless teachings with new
generations of believers, he began salvaging as many
cassette tapes of his dad's sermons as he could gather, as
well as many reel-to-reel tapes (the primary recording
mediums of that era). He listened to the tapes carefully,
took extensive notes, and drafted 365 two-page
devotionals—all exclusively from Jamie's spoken
words.

After 10 years, he finally completed the project. Then the compilation was carefully and thoughtfully edited by his wife, Michele, a professional book editor with scores of books to her credit.

As you will discover, Jamie's teachings are as fresh and as relevant today as when he first spoke them—if not more so. The devotions you are about to read are deep, challenging, insightful, encouraging, authentic, and sometimes humorous. Our hope is that you won't settle for this small sampling of 25 devotions—that after you get a taste, you will want to move on to the full meal!

Meeting God at Every Corner is no small, light, or inconsequential book. It is a legacy volume. Not only does it include one two-page devotion for every day of the year; it also includes meticulously curated indexes that reference all the scriptures mentioned, biblical figures noted, and topics discussed within its pages.

As an added bonus, we have digitally connected each devotion to the original sermon spoken by Jamie from which it is derived. You can listen to these teachings for free by going to the online devotional calendar found at www.JamieBuckinghamMinistries.com/devotionals.

It has been our sincere honor to compile this work and make it available to all who have ears to hear—all whom the Father draws, all who desire to know more of our Lord Jesus Christ and His precious Holy Spirit. Jamie Buckingham sought to live a Spirit-led life, and he devoted his life to teaching and encouraging others to be guided and empowered by the Spirit of God. *Meeting God at Every Corner* is the culmination and capstone of life's work.

The full volume of *Meeting God at Every Corner* is available through all the normal online booksellers. However, if you wish to order copies directly from us, please use the form at the end of this book, or visit our website: www.JamieBuckinghamMinistries.com. Many other books and resources by Jamie Buckingham can be found on the website, as well.

If you have any comments or questions, please reach out to us at bruce@rlmin.com.

In His love and grace,

Bruce and Michele Buckingham
Risky Living Ministries,
Palm Bay, Florida

January 1
Meeting God at Every Corner

"Do not be afraid, for I am with you." (Isaiah 43:5)

I have spoken to many individuals who, for various reasons, are very apprehensive about the future. They seem to be constantly worrying about this or that. But mostly they are anxious about things they have no control over. They wonder what might happen if they lose their job, or their marriage falls apart, or a loved one gets seriously sick—or worse, dies.

People ask me all the time, "What can I do? How can I stop worrying about the future?"

My answer, quite simply, is this: "The only thing you can do when it comes to the future is to trust God."

I tell people that God knows our future, and He has promised to be there when we arrive at it. He knows our worries and our concerns, but He also knows where we are heading. He knows what is around every corner we will turn in life. So, trust Him!

There is nothing that could happen to you that God has not seen before. No matter where God leads, others have gone that way before you. In fact, others have been where you *are*, and they have been where you are *going*. As King Solomon said, there is really nothing new under the sun.

God is the same yesterday, today and forever. There may be a lot we don't know about the future; but with God's grace and help, we can make it, just as others did before us. God is there for us, just as He was for them.

I am convinced that whatever happens to us as Christians, wherever God takes us, we will come out on the other side better than we could have ever anticipated or expected.

The word I am hearing for today is faithfulness. Sure, there is uncertainty in the world, but there is also God's faithfulness. There is uncertainty on man's part, but there is faithfulness on God's part. As the song goes, "Great is Thy faithfulness, morning by morning new mercies I see."

God will not let His people down. His promises are true. He does not lie like men do. He does not do things out of self-interest like men do. God is faithful, and He has made promises to us. He will meet us at every turn.

Life is filled with change—with corners that must be turned. But I'm convinced that if you are walking with God, you can be sure that, around each corner, there is something glorious waiting for you. Every time you make a new turn, life is better in some way than it was before, because God works all things together for good for those who are called according to His purpose.

It doesn't matter what happens to you, because God is already out there in front of you. He'll meet you when you turn that corner. He'll meet you in your times of crisis and in your times of change. He'll meet you when you get married, when you have children, when you change jobs, or when you move across the country. He'll meet you when you are sick, and He will be there, on the other side, waiting for you, when you die.

Great is God's faithfulness! Because of it, we do not have to fear the corners in life—not even the greatest corner, death. We will simply meet Him there, as we always have in life, and move on into what comes next.

Yes, the future is uncertain. But God is in charge of this world. He is faithful. And He will meet you at every corner. Don't be afraid!

January 15
Half-Baked Christians

"Ephraim mixes with the nations; Ephraim is a flat cake not turned over." (Hosea 7:8)

I spent some time recently in the Sinai Desert with some Bedouin people who showed me how they bake unleavened bread. Using the same procedure Moses used, they took flour, salt and water and made dough. Then they laid it directly on coals made of dried camel dung. When one side was thoroughly baked, they turned the bread over and baked the other side, making sure the whole thing was cooked through and through. Cooking on one side only, they told me, was totally insufficient.

When the children of Israel entered the Promised Land, Ephraim, one of the twelve tribes of Israel, failed to comply with a decree from God prohibiting all Israelites from mixing with and marrying the local Canaanites. The tribe of Ephraim entered the land, but they didn't follow all the way through in their dedication to God.

The prophet Hosea spoke of this when he said Ephraim was like a flat cake, or bread, that had not been turned over in the final baking process. Because of the sin of the tribe of Ephraim, the resulting people—we know them as the Samaritans—became a thorn in the side of the Israelites for centuries to come.

Paul speaks of this same type of behavior in a Christian context: believers not following all the way through in their walk with Christ. In Colossians 2 he states that we are not to live our lives dependent upon human tradition or the basic principles of this world; rather, we should depend fully upon Christ. We should live continually in Christ, seeking His guidance day by day.

We cannot walk with one foot in the world and one foot in the kingdom of God. Failure to continue to live fully in Christ—failure to continually be filled with the

Holy Spirit—creates "half-baked" Christians: cooked on one side but raw on the other.

How many of us have only entered part-way into our experience with God, stopping short of allowing ourselves to be turned over and exposed to the fire of the Holy Spirit?

How easy it is for us to enter into the Christian experience but fail to expose all sides of ourselves to the cleansing fire of God! We talk like we are fully devoted to Christ, but we have failed marriages; we are foolish with our money and resources; we don't seek Christ to guide our lives on a daily basis.

When you fail to turn over every aspect of your life to Christ—or worse, when you go backwards and pull parts of yourself back from His control—you are half-baked! You may appear good and righteous on one side, but look behind you. You are half-baked, not done; never fully exposed to the fire of the Spirit.

It's time to get honest. Have you become dull in your enthusiasm for Christ? Are the things of this world eroding the foundations of your Christian faith? Are you listening to the counsel of this world rather than to the wisdom of God?

Has the Word of God somehow been drained from you, so that you are only half-baked? Are you like the tribe of Ephraim—a flat cake not turned over, not baked through on every side, in every way?

I believe God wants a deeper commitment from us. Let's live each day fully dedicated to our daily walk with Christ, so that one day, when the Master comes along, digging around in the coals, He will see us and say, "Well done, good and faithful servant. Well done—on both sides."

January 23
Airborne with God

Provide for those who grieve in Zion—bestow on them a
crown of beauty instead of ashes, the oil of gladness
instead of mourning, and a garment of praise instead of
a spirit of despair. (Isaiah 61:3)

Before I earned my private pilot's license, I thought
an airplane flew by being pushed up from below, as the
air passed beneath its wings. In pilot training, however, I
quickly learned that is not the case. As air rapidly passes
over the top of the wings, a low-pressure area is created
above them, and the plane is actually lifted off the ground.
An airplane wing is heavy by nature, but when it is angled
correctly, the wind passing over it becomes a powerful
lifting force that weight cannot hold down.

Praise is like that in our spiritual lives. The Book of
Isaiah tells us that praise is like a beautiful garment from
God that we choose to put on. In the presence of praise,
despair's tattered rags fall away. Praise is also like the
wind across our wings. When our hearts are full of praise,
we become airborne, not from our own doings or strivings
that push up from below, but rather from God giving us
lift from above.

We can't pump ourselves up, like a jack pumping up
a flat tire. It doesn't work that way. We can't generate our
own lifting power. Only God can lift us beyond the
bounds of our earthly pain and despair.

Even as Christians, we have times in our lives when
we feel great heaviness—like ice on our spiritual wings.
We feel grounded, stuck in the hangar. Thankfully, the
Holy Spirit is with us to tell us when there is a buildup of
ice, or anything else, that might keep us from flying
safely. He is faithful to keep watch over the status of our
spiritual wings and to help us do whatever is necessary to
prepare us again for flight.

There are also times when we, as Christians, experience difficult circumstances—like strong headwinds blowing so hard at us, we think they might blow us away altogether. But all pilots know that headwinds assist in getting a plane off the ground. In our spiritual lives, it is often the contrary headwinds that help lift us off the tarmac and get us moving upward and onward.

Of course, most of us would rather have the winds just blow us down the runways of life, pushing us from behind. We don't want to face into them. We don't see the wisdom of turning into a headwind, as a pilot does; it seems too difficult and contradictory to our purposes.

But as a pilot knows, the problem with taking off downwind is that he will never build up adequate airspeed to get his plane off the ground. He may instead run into the fence at the end of the runway. A good pilot intentionally faces his airplane into the headwind, because he knows that the winds blowing toward him—passing rapidly across the top of his wings—will lift him off the ground. And once he is airborne, he has the freedom to go in any direction he wants.

We don't like to face those contrary winds that blow against us. But stop and think about it. The problem is not with the wind; the problem is with ourselves. We spend so much time trying to circumvent difficult circumstances in our lives! We need to realize it is God who sends the headwinds, so that we can be lifted up. He has built us in such a way that, when the headwinds blow against us, we fly—as long as we're facing in the right direction.

Circumstances and struggles are God's way of getting you airborne. So stop avoiding them. Face the headwinds and go full throttle into them, giving praise to God, and He will lift you up.

January 24
A Burning Bush Encounter

God said to Moses, "I AM WHO I AM. This is what you
are to say to the Israelites: 'I AM has sent me to you.'"
(Exodus 3:14)

According to the Book of Exodus, God spoke to Moses from a burning bush and told him his life's purpose. Moses was a man who had been languishing in the desert seemingly without purpose for 40 years. He knew about God; he knew something of his Jewish heritage. But when the Lord spoke to him unexpectedly that day in the desert, his initial reaction was to question not only his newly-revealed purpose but also God's identity.

What is your purpose in life? Do you know? For Moses, his purpose became known to him once he came to know who God is—once he met God on a deep, personal level. Like Moses, we will find our purpose only when we come to know who God is through a deep and personal encounter with Him.

And like Moses, even after that encounter, we won't live out our purpose without struggle. After Moses met God in the burning bush, he still had all the same faults and problems he'd had before. He still struggled with doubt and unbelief. The difference was, now he knew his goal in life. His purpose had been revealed by God Himself—and that was a game-changer.

It is interesting that, despite the incredible revelation of God in the burning bush, Moses demanded more specifics. He wanted God to define Himself, to reveal Himself further. A bush that burned but was not consumed was not enough for him. But to Moses' question, "What is Your name?" God responded not so much with a name as with a statement: "I am Who I am."

15

I believe God wants to bring us to the place where we don't need to know His name beyond "I am"—where we don't need to know anything other than the fact that He is, and He has called us into our ultimate purpose in life. The Scriptures are filled with names of God; but perhaps God wants us to know Him and accept Him simply because He is Who He is.

"I am" is the first-person present tense of the verb "to be." All being rests in God, the Creator of the heavens and the earth. Who are we to ask, "Who are You? What is Your name?" Don't we understand the true greatness of the God we serve? Why do we have to define Him, name Him, or put man-made titles on Him?

The disciples tried to place titles on Jesus, but He refused to be labeled. Rabbi? Prophet? Jesus gently told them they could call Him "Son of Man." That's not much of a title, is it? What Jesus was really saying was, "Just accept Me and receive Me, and you will know who I am. My name will be written on your hearts."

As believers, we should not be limited by the world's demand to place definitions or titles or labels on everyone and everything under the sun. God is not bound by worldly definitions, and we are not to be bound by the ways of the world.

Have you had a burning bush experience? Are you fulfilling the purpose God gave you, or are you still in the desert, arguing with God and making demands? God wants each of us to be willing and ready to follow His voice, even if it comes from a burning bush. That ought to be all we need to know who He is; because, after all, He is writing His name on our hearts.

February 1
Back to the Garden

Now the Lord had planted a garden in the east, in Eden;
and there he put the man he had formed. (Genesis 2:8)

The ultimate goal of all our Christian growth—our diligent Bible studies, our prayer and fasting, our relationships and fellowships—is that we enter into a very deep, personal, intimate relationship with the Lord Jesus Christ.

Jesus is God's projection of Himself to us here on Earth. Our relationship with Him is a mystical, communal relationship. It defies any definition or description, because it is different for each us; after all, no two of us are alike. But through this experience of ever-deepening relationship, Jesus becomes very close to us. We have fellowship with Him; and through Him, with God the Father. As we walk with Him daily, God brings to us restoration of a kind that only He can accomplish. One part of this is restoration of our earthly relationships. This does not always mean that our relationships with people become as they once were; that is not always possible. But it does mean there will be healing and restoring of our broken, hurting hearts.

The main restoration God seeks, however, is in our spiritual relationship with Him. Our heavenly Father wants our relationship with Him to be as it once was, way back in the Garden of Eden.

The purpose of Jesus coming to Earth goes back to the prophecy found in Joel chapter 2: God will restore to us everything the locusts have eaten. That prophecy has to do with more than just the grain fields in Israel. It has to do with our spiritual relationship with God—the relationship that was destroyed when Adam and Eve broke fellowship with God in the garden.

Before they sinned, Adam and Eve knew God. They had perfect communion with Him. As the Bible puts it, they did not worry about their nakedness. God wants that kind of relationship restored with each of us. He wants us to know Him and walk with Him the way Adam and Eve did.

God's desire has always been for us to know Him intimately. On this, He has never wavered. That is what restoration is all about. Because of sin, man's relationship with God was broken. But God set a plan in motion, and through Jesus Christ, the potential for relationship has been restored.

Jesus is the way, the truth, and the life, and no man comes into a relationship with the Father but through Him. If we really believe this, then we can have communion with God the Father. We can walk with Him. We can know Him, and He will know us and direct us and guide us. He will meet our needs, and He will bless us.

Because of Christ, the relationship that Adam and Eve had with God in the Garden is available to us today. The angel with the flaming sword who was set at Eden's gate to turn everyone away is no longer there to keep us out. He is only there to keep out those who are not under the blood of Christ. Everything that was destroyed by sin is now restored by the blood. Through Jesus, we can go back to God's original intention. We can go back to the beginning.

Ask the Holy Spirit to bring to mind areas of your life that need restoration, including broken relationships with relatives or friends. God wants to restore our relationships with one another, just as He wants to restore our relationship with Him. Wait quietly before Him, and He will give you grace to forgive. He will heal your heart. He will draw you close to Himself.

Listen for His voice. Even now He invites you to walk with Him daily in the garden, where His presence is as near as your breath and His blessings abound.

18

February 2
Senior Saints

Therefore we do not lose heart. Though outwardly we are wasting away, yet inwardly we are being renewed day by day.(2 Corinthians 4:16)

Above my mirror I have taped an old saying: "All things are changing, and we are changing with them."

I have looked at that message over the years; and as I grow older, I recognize its truth more and more. I am changing, and that's not bad. In fact, it's quite good, considering the alternative. I believe it is God's plan and purpose for all of us to grow old and change. But it is not God's purpose for us to grow old and stop serving Him.

Everything changes, because our God is a God of change. Every time we find God characterized in the Bible, it is in the context of movement. There is nothing stationary about God. He is always progressing, always moving forward.

As Christians, we can be confident that everything in our lives is moving forward, too, toward a predetermined goal that God has planned and established for us. We are not just floating along in life without direction or purpose. We are part of something God is doing, regardless of our age or physical condition. We are part of a preordained plan for history.

Whatever our age, each of us counts in that plan. We have purpose and value. God has something out there that only we can do, and if we don't do it, it will never get done. We are here for a purpose, whether we're 18 or 80.

Once we grasp this, we have no reason to ever feel useless or depressed. We're *not* bobbing aimlessly on a dead sea. Our best seafaring days are *not* behind us! The wind is still blowing across the waters; all we need to do is raise our sails.

19

Consider that all of your life up to this point has been preparatory for the big thing God has purposed for you to do. Ask Him for the vision to see it. Ask Him for a word that says, "See this, here? This is for you."

One of the great tragedies in this world is that, too often, older people are put on a shelf. Society tells them their productive years are over, and the only place for them is out to pasture. But the truth is, our senior saints are here because they have so much to give. They are here to both lead and to serve. They are here because they have a wealth of wisdom to share with the rest of us—wisdom that only comes through the living of years.

If you've reached a certain age, I want to encourage you: Don't just sit on the porch in your rocking chair and say, "I'm done. All I want to do now is enjoy retirement." If you do that, you are cutting yourself off from the will of God. There is no place in His Word where He tells His people to retire. It's just not part of His plan.

God needs you during *all* the years you're alive on this earth. In fact, He needs you now more than He ever needed you in all your life. It doesn't matter how old you are; you have reason to be excited about your future!

So put up your sail and catch the wind of the Spirit. Get involved in your church. Get involved in the lives of the people around you. Be creative and productive up to the day God calls you home. And never let your age stop you from doing what God is calling you to do.

February 5
A People Who Hear God's Voice

"And I tell you that you are Peter, and on this rock I will build my church, and the gates of Hades will not overcome it." (Matthew 16:18)

When Jesus told Peter, "On this rock I will build My church," what is the rock He was talking about? I believe the rock is "revelation knowledge"—the word of the Lord. The Scriptures tell us that the church is made up of people who hear God. We are simply a group of people whose hearts and minds and spiritual ears are tuned to God. That's all.

The word for "church" in Greek is *ecclesia*, meaning those who are "called out." Separate. Different. And the reason we are different is because we hear God's voice.

God is talking to everyone. Romans 1 makes it clear that God communicates with the whole world through many means, including creation itself. But only those who confess that Jesus is the Son of God—only those who call Him Lord—are able to hear His voice.

The *ecclesia* walks not according to the sounds of the world, or the whims of government, or the clamor of society. We walk according to the word of God. Moment by moment, we hear Him and respond to Him. We listen for the voice of His Holy Spirit within us, and we do only what He tells us to do.

Have you noticed that Jesus never set up a specific structure for His church? He never established a doctrinal creed or an order of service. It was not His intention to pull together as many people as possible to get up on Sundays and "go to church." What He wanted —what He still wants—is a fellowship of men and women who hear His voice; who stand on His Word; who are filled with the Holy Spirit; and who allow God alone to direct their lives.

21

Ecclesia. It's an exciting life that the world outside of Jesus Christ just doesn't understand. But hearing and following the voice of God is the only thing that will keep you out of hell. And it's the only thing that will give you true joy, abundance, and fulfillment here on Earth.

Every child of Jesus hears God. When we become new creations in Christ, "ears to hear" are standard equipment. "My sheep will hear My voice," He said. Of course, sometimes we don't like what we hear, and we choose to go our own way. But that's a whole different story!

Right now, I want to encourage you to hear God for yourself. Resist those people who think they are speaking for God to you. You don't need anyone to tell you how to live your life, when God Himself is speaking to you directly. Just take the time to listen for His voice and, when you hear Him, do what He says.

Of course, hearing God for yourself does not mean walking through life alone. God wants us to walk with our brothers and sisters in the church, too. We may not all be walking at the same pace, but we *are* walking in the same direction. We're on the same journey, and we have this in common: we are taking our direction from God instead of the world.

As God's *ecclesia*, we are filled with the same Holy Spirit. We have the same authority over the devil. We have the same orders to go into all the world, be a witness for Jesus, and make disciples. We have the same high call to join with the Lord and one another in building the kingdom of God.

Let's agree together to be different than the world. Let's be a people who love one another; who build each other up rather than tear each other down; who walk, not in conformity, but in the unity of the Spirit. Let's be a people who hear God's voice. Let's be the *ecclesia* of God.

February 13
A Life of Creativity and Adventure

"But my righteous one will live by faith. And if he shrinks back, I will not be pleased with him". But we are not of those who shrink back and are destroyed, but of those who believe and are saved. (Hebrews 10:38-39)

God has placed within each of us natural drives or instincts that cause us to be who we are as individuals. We have a drive for security and for recognition. We have a need to love and to be loved. We also have a drive to be creative and to seek adventure.

Our drive to be creative, for example, is God-derived, because it is the very nature of God to be creative. We fulfill a need within us when we bring new things into being. Some people are artists or sculptors; others construct buildings or build bridges; some folks get joy from decorating their homes. Farmers plant crops and watch them grow; doctors stitch up wounds then step back and watch them heal. Creativity can be manifested in a thousand different ways.

All these drives, in various combinations, control most of our life patterns. And since they are given to us by a loving heavenly Father, they can only truly be fulfilled through a relationship with Him.

If you try to fulfill your God-given drives outside of a personal relationship with the Father, they are going to veer off course and eventually fly out of control, because they are influenced by the world rather than by God. That's how you end up with a politician who uses his power selfishly to build his own kingdom on Earth. It's how you end up with a man whose God-given sex drive leads him to turn to pornography—or worse, a sex crime. A genuine unfulfilled need gets perverted when its fulfillment is sought outside of a relationship with the Lord.

All our needs and drives can be met only in Jesus. We are created to find satisfaction only in relationship with Him. Satisfied people don't live out-of-control lives; they live lives controlled by the Spirit of God.

What about our drive for adventure? It, too, is a noble, God-given instinct, placed inside us by an adventurous God. After all, God created the earth from nothing; then He put people on it and said, "I will run the risk of letting them loose on the planet." What an adventure He set in motion, for Himself and for us!

But what if you try to fulfill your drive for adventure by going to Las Vegas and gambling away all your money? That's one example of how you can degrade or misappropriate a godly natural drive by seeking its fulfillment through the world rather than through the Lord.

We have been made in the image of God. Just as God engaged His infinite character of creativity to create the world, He has placed in each of us a desire to create. In a similar way, He endowed each of us with a drive for adventure, out of the infinite character of adventure that He possesses in Himself.

Pursuing adventure and creating new things are inherently risky enterprises. That's why faith in Christ is an absolute necessity in the life of every believer. God calls us to step out and take risks. The Bible calls it "living by faith." If we choose to walk through this world without a relationship with Jesus—without faith—we will be lost.

If we don't live by faith, we won't take risks. And if we won't take risks, we can't really live.

None of us knows what tomorrow holds. But when we know the God who holds our tomorrows, we can fully embrace the adventure of life, confident that all our God-given desires and drives will be satisfied in Him.

24

February 17
A Risky Walk

*Be kind and compassionate to one another, forgiving
each other, just as in Christ God forgave you.
(Ephesians 4:32)*

I wrote a book several years ago called *Risky Living*.
Even after it was published, I continued to learn more
about what "risky living" really means.

As believers, we often like to set risky goals,
impossible goals. We like to dream impossible dreams.
And that is good, because you can never achieve anything
of great significance without dreaming to do the
seemingly impossible.

But I have learned that it is not really the goals or
dreams that are risky. The thing that is truly risky—the
thing that will cost you everything—is the actual walking
out of those goals or dreams. Anybody can dream.
Anyone can set impossible goals and then begin moving
one step at a time toward them. But the dream is not what
is risky. The risky part is acting on your dream and
walking it out for the rest of your life.

As I've continued to consider the meaning of "risky
living" in my own life, I want to share five truths that have
become meaningful to me:

1. *How a task is done is more important than
whether it is completed or not.* Of course, God wants me
to strive toward the completion of the tasks He has put
before me. But how I go about doing these tasks and my
attitude while doing them is far more important to God
than the actual completion of them. Some tasks might
never be completed—at least, not by me—and that is
okay, because God is looking on my heart as I work
toward their completion. God is far more interested in my
motives than He is my accomplishments.

25

2. *It is more important to be kind than to be right.* The Bible commands us to be kind to other people. To God, my character is more important than my charisma, my talent, or even my "rightness." If I march through life always stepping on people because I'm convinced I'm right—well, that would not be kind, and God would look harshly upon it. God is very interested in how I behave toward others.

3. *It is possible to be supernaturally led and protected by God and still miss His ultimate purpose.* The perfect example is the children of Israel in the wilderness. For 40 years in the desert, God led them and provided for them, but they were 180 degrees out of His will. It is so easy to be deceived into thinking you are in God's will simply because you have all the stuff you need. I've learned that I can't determine if I'm in God's will based on outward circumstances or prosperity. If I am blessed financially and have good health, so what? A lot of Satan's people are healthy and have lots of money. It is possible for me to have the blessings of God and still miss His purpose.

4. *The closer I get to God, the more I need to lean on my brothers and sisters in Christ.* It's actually impossible to get close to God without getting close to the body of Christ at the same time. We're in this thing together, and we need each other. As I seek God's will, set big goals, and walk out the risky life of an ever-deepening relationship with God, I have an increasing need for deep fellowship with God's people around me.

5. *The most important thing in my life is the complete lordship of Jesus Christ.* That is God's end purpose for me, and for all of us, during our time on Earth. He wants us to come fully under the lordship of His Son, Jesus, and become like Him. Then the end is not an end at all; it's the beginning of all that God has planned for us in eternal life.

March 7
Your Shadow Ministry

People brought the sick into the streets and laid them on beds and mats so that at least Peter's shadow might fall on some of them as he passed by. (Acts 5:15)

Several years ago, I was climbing Mt. Sinai, doing research for a book I was writing. My little group of men rose early in the morning so we could be at the summit for the sunrise. As we climbed the mountain in the dark, a group of ten or so dark-skinned men wearing sandals and loin cloths came up from behind us and swiftly passed us.

When we reached the mountaintop, we saw the other men gathered for a prayer meeting, singing in a language we didn't understand. An Australian missionary was with them, and I asked him about the group. "These men are New Guinea Aborigines," he said, "the first of their tribe to ever visit Israel. They are believers, and they are here to see if the places mentioned in the Bible are real."

The Australian went on to explain that he had once been an outlaw biker, but his life had been changed when he read a book about God written by an American author. He became a Christian and, eventually, a missionary in New Guinea, where he was instrumental in leading hundreds of tribespeople to the Lord.

"You're an American," he said. "Have you ever heard of this author? His name is Jamie Buckingham."

I said, "You're not going to believe what I'm about to tell you. I'm Jamie Buckingham."

He was amazed, and we all rejoiced! Then one of the Aborigines, the old tribal chief, spoke something to me in his native language. The Australian translated. "Thank you for casting your shadow over us in New Guinea," the chief had said.

Immediately I recalled the scripture in Acts chapter 5, when the Apostle Peter's shadow fell on the sick people who lined the streets of Jerusalem as he passed by, and they were healed. Peter did not reach out intentionally to touch and heal anyone; but because he was facing toward Jesus and walking in obedience to God, even his shadow carried the power of the Holy Spirit.

All I had done was use the small gift God had given me to write a book. That manuscript was then edited, printed, published, and distributed by various other people who were using their small gifts. Each of us, in our own ways, were simply being obedient. And the shadow went out across the world. The book found its way to Australia and into the hands of an outlaw biker who was touched by God, became a believer, and ministered God's love to a tribe of Aborigines in New Guinea, who now stood with me, praising God, on the summit of Mt. Sinai.

I wonder if so much of what we do in life that seems insignificant to us may not be, in fact, the most important things we ever do. Maybe the most significant things are the things whose impact we never even know about.

If you look back over your life, you will most likely recall people whose shadows have touched you and blessed you. Because of them, you are who you are today. Now, as you use your small gifts in the Lord's service, your shadow is falling on untold numbers of others. God is blessing and healing them, not because you are intentionally reaching out to touch them, but because you are walking in obedience to the Lord.

God is using your "shadow ministry" and mine to build His church, and the gates of hell will not prevail against it! Just keep moving forward with your face toward Jesus. Be obedient. Let your shadow fall where it will. God will do the rest.

March 8
Ordinary People

*As Jesus was getting into the boat, the man who had
been demon-possessed begged to go with him. Jesus did
not let him, but said, "Go home to your family and tell
them how much the Lord has done for you, and how he
has had mercy on you." (Mark 5:18-19)*

The kingdom of God is not carried on the shoulders
of giants. It is carried on the shoulders of ordinary folks
like you and me, empowered by an extraordinary God.

Any kingdom work that is meaningful and lasting is
going to happen in the local body of Christ. Only there
can we come face to face with one another and place an
arm around each other. Only there can we minister
directly to our family members, neighbors, and friends.

I praise God for big TV ministries and globe-trotting
preachers. They have brought the Word of God to untold
numbers. But nothing substitutes for coming face to face
with someone Jesus loves and through whom Jesus is
working.

In Acts 16 we read about a woman named Lydia who
was a dealer in purple cloth from the city of Thyatira. The
Bible says she was a worshiper of God. Neither Paul nor
any of the apostles had been to Philippi before that time,
as far as we know. So, how had she heard about the one
true God of the universe? The book of Acts does not say.
From history, however, we know that traders in cloth,
such as Lydia, often traveled to the Decapolis because it
was a well-known source for high-quality purple dye. It is
entirely possible that Lydia made several trips to this area.

In Mark chapter 5—many years before Acts 16—we
read about Jesus going into the Decapolis region and
delivering a man from multiple demons. Afterwards, the
man begged to follow Jesus, but Jesus said no. Instead, He
told him to go home and tell his family and friends about

the wonderful miracle he had experienced. The grateful man did more than that; he "went away and began to tell in the Decapolis how much Jesus had done for him."

Could it be that Lydia, in her travels to the region, heard about Jesus from this formerly demon-possessed man, then returned to her own city a believer? It's a plausible assumption.

Because of this man's obedience, Paul and Silas had a home to stay in during their visit to Philippi. Because of his obedience, the gospel is ours today. A man we know nothing more about—only that he experienced a touch from Jesus and told others about it—shared his testimony with a woman named Lydia, who in turn opened her home to the Apostle Paul, who then used that home as the base for his ministry to the Western world.

The kingdom of God does not rest on the shoulders of giants. It is carried on the shoulders of ordinary people who tell their family members, friends, and neighbors about what Jesus has done for them.

There is no force as powerful as the name of Jesus Christ in the mouth of a believer. You may not be called to travel the world and reach millions for the gospel; not many are, and that's okay. Your task may be to stay home and do whatever your hand finds to do—and to do it with all your might, as a witness for Christ. Your task may be to simply be the presence of Jesus to whomever you meet, right where you are. God will do the rest, and He will get the glory.

So, fasten your eyes on the Lord, ordinary people! Be obedient to Him, and He will do extraordinary things through you.

March 14
Don't Waste Your Pain

Praise be to the God and Father of our Lord Jesus
Christ, the Father of compassion and the God of all
comfort, who comforts us in all our troubles, so that we
can comfort those in any trouble with the comfort we
ourselves have received from God. (2 Corinthians 1:3-4)

Do you believe there is a purpose for your pain? Do
you believe God has a plan in the midst of your distress
or despair? As Christians, it is important for us to
remember that God never allows anything to come into
our lives that does not pass first through His loving hands.

You may think, "But there are a lot of things that
come into my life that I'm not sure have passed first
through God's hands—if He even knows about them at
all!" So, you go knocking on His door to ask Him if He is
aware of your situation. "God, do you know that this is
happening right now?" Or, "God, in case you forgot about
me and what I'm going through, let me remind you . . ."

God is both loving and omniscient. He knows about
all our troubles. He is fully aware of each and every one
of our situations. Even though we know this, we still ask
questions, and they usually begin with "Why?" "Why,
Lord? Why me? Why this? Why now?"

I can give you at least one answer from the words of
Paul in 2 Corinthians chapter 1. The purpose for the pain,
misery, and suffering we experience is to prepare us to
"comfort those in any trouble with the comfort we
ourselves have received from God." In the process of
being comforted ourselves and then comforting others,
our own relationship with God is deepened, and we have
the opportunity to lead others into a personal relationship
with the God of all comfort.

Paul goes on to say, "If we are distressed, it is for
your comfort and salvation, which produces in you patient

31

endurance." What produces patient endurance? Comfort, which is preceded by suffering. That means that if you walk through the purpose God has ordained for your suffering, not only will you gain patience and endurance, but you will experience glory on the other side. And the comfort of God will be with you all the way through.

If you haven't experienced pain or rejection, you can't really know what it's like. If you haven't been thrown out of a place where you expected to be loved, you can't know what it's like to have a loved one turn their back on you. Unless you have walked through your own emotional hurt, or financial hardship, or poor health, you can't know what it's like to suffer in these ways.

But Jesus experienced the fullest extent of suffering when He was on the earth. He is able to empathize with us in every way. His desire is that, when we go through tough times—as all of us will—we come out on the other side willing and able to comfort others who are experiencing the same things we did.

All of us need someone who understands our hurts, our frustrations, our physical ailments. We all need someone who has been there before us, who can simply put an arm around us and say, "God will see you through, just as He saw me through."

The fact is, life can be hard. Chronic pain, rejection, and difficult circumstances are the devil's tools to get your eyes off God and onto yourself. But if you will, instead, focus on God, believing that He is "the God of all comfort, who comforts us in all our troubles," then the purpose of your pain will be fulfilled.

Our God is a God of miracles. That means there is always hope, no matter how dark or painful life gets. So, don't waste your pain! As you go through suffering, allow God, through His Holy Spirit, to comfort you. Then, go and comfort others with the same comfort you have received. In that process, healing will come.

April 1
Are All the Children In?

On my bed I remember you; I think of you through the
watches of the night. Because you are my help, I sing in
the shadow of your wings. (Psalm 63:6)

A while ago I visited my mother in her nursing home
in Vero Beach. She is 92, and her body and mind are
gradually failing. Each time I visit, she tells me she wants
to go home. I know what she means.

That afternoon I tried to tell her about an experience
we'd had at the church service that morning. I thought she
would be interested in knowing that one of her great-
grandsons had been baptized. But she had a hard time
understanding what I was telling her. She couldn't grasp
the details of my story. She would hear bits and pieces,
then they would slip away from her. She began to cry. "I
just can't remember," she said.

"It's okay, mother," I told her. "It's alright." Then I
read to her from Isaiah 43: "Forget the former things; do
not dwell on the past. See, I am doing a new thing! Now
it springs up; do you not perceive it?"

"Mother," I said, "what is *about* to happen is so much
greater than what *has* happened. It doesn't make any
difference what you can or cannot remember. What has
happened, happened. What is about to happen is more
wonderful, and it is in God's hands. That's the important
thing."

Then she looked at me and asked the question I
remember her father, old Colonel Thompson, asking back
in her childhood home in Winchester, Kentucky. When I
was a kid, we would visit that big old house. It had nine
bedrooms. I remember spending nights there and hearing
him shout out late at night to my grandmother, "Mama,
are all the children in?" He wasn't going to go to sleep
until he knew where all the kids were.

That afternoon in the nursing home, my mother had a flashback to her father calling out in the night, and she asked, "Jamie, are all the children in?"

I realized then that when you get to the end of life, most things just don't make any difference. Nothing matters except knowing that all the children are safely in, all have accepted Jesus, all are walking in the light of the kingdom of God. What is more important than knowing your loved ones are going to heaven? What is more important than knowing you are going to see them again someday?

At the end of your days, nothing else matters. All the armies that have marched, all the governments that have deliberated, all the rockets that have flown in outer space, all the medicine, all the technology, all the knowledge— none of it matters. The only thing that matters is knowing that all the children are in. That's what counts.

"Are all the children in?" she asked me again.

"Yes, Mother," I said gently. "As far as I know, all the kids are in. They're safe. It's okay to go to sleep now."

That's what God's message is all about. Jesus came to gather His family together and bring us into His house. We may come from different backgrounds, different nationalities, different ethnic origins. But those things are not what make us family. What makes us family is that each of us has put our faith in the Savior, Jesus Christ; and we can say with one voice, "Jesus is Lord."

April 8
The God of Resurrection

"If someone dies, will they live again?" (Job 14:14)

We all have dreams—dreams for ourselves, dreams for our children, dreams for our communities, dreams for our nation. But these are temporal dreams, earthbound dreams. There is one dream, however, that is bigger and grander than all the others. It was first voiced as a question by Job when he asked, "If a man die, will he live again?"

We all dream about life beyond this earthly life, and the fulfillment of that dream is possible because of Jesus. The Scripture states in John 1:12, "Yet to all who did receive him, to those who believed in his name, he gave the right to become children of God." By accepting Jesus as Savior, we become children of the Most High God, Creator of heaven and earth. Victory over life and victory over death become ours.

When all we see around us is defeat, however, it can be hard to believe that victory is coming.

The Bible tells us about that Sunday morning after the crucifixion, when the two women went to the tomb of Jesus to anoint His body for burial. The women saw that the stone had been rolled away, and the body of their Lord was gone. They were devastated. But at that very moment, two angels stood beside them and said, "Why do you look for the living among the dead? He is not here. He is risen."

Have you ever noticed how God uses ordinary events to bring extraordinary things to pass? How He uses ordinary people to do extraordinary works? These two ordinary women went to the tomb to do what was ordinary within their tradition when a loved one died. All the dreams they'd had as followers of Jesus had been dashed at the crucifixion; but then something extraordinary happened.

35

We don't always see what God has in store for us. We worry when things don't go the way we planned or hoped for. But the fact that we are alive today, meeting together in the name of Jesus, is testimony that God is in control of both life and death, and He does indeed care for our wellbeing.

Soon after I moved my family to Florida in the late 1960s, I was fired from my position as pastor of a small church. I thought it was the end of everything. I didn't have anywhere to go or anything to do. One day I was a pastor with a secure salary, and the next day I was out.

Then a small group from the church agreed to gather with me in the park. It was the Sunday before Easter, Palm Sunday. There were about sixty of us including children—five of whom were my own. We brought food and invited friends. The idea was to form a new church. I tried to sound excited, but inside I was miserable and discouraged. I was beaten down by life and by my own sin. I was as near to quitting as I have ever been.

It was a crucifixion experience for me, and at that moment, I had no hope. But today I look back, and I see with great clarity that a resurrection soon followed. Today, I see God's hand on my life, even when I thought He had left me. I know now, without a doubt, that God was and still is in control. He never left me. He just had other plans for me.

So, be encouraged. All the disappointments you feel today, all the things you wanted to happen that aren't happening, all the things you didn't want to happen that are—they are not the end. If you've reached the point where life seems to be crushing you down, and you wonder if God is really there and if He really cares, remember: our God resurrects! He does it His way, and He does it in His time. But He is Lord, and He is alive.

Not only will He see you through the darkest of days, He will make your life new. Victory is yours, because you are a child of God. Resurrection is coming.

April 12
How to Live with Bad Decisions

David said to Abigail, "Praise be to the Lord, the God of Israel, who has sent you today to meet me. May you be blessed for your good judgement." (1 Samuel 25:32-33)

In 1 Samuel 25, we read about a woman named Abigail. She was a smart, beautiful, loyal wife who happened to be married to a worthless, drunken husband named Nabal. One day, Nabal infuriated David, the soon-to-be king, by refusing a simple request from David's servants. So, David set out to confront Nabal and even threatened to kill him. But before he could reach Nabal, David was intercepted by Abigail, who used wisdom and diplomacy to persuade David to turn around and spare her foolish husband.

In that encounter, David recognized that Abigail was special. As a woman of honor, she had decided to stand by her vows to Nabal, even though she knew marrying him had been the biggest mistake of her life.

The next day Nabal had a heart attack, and within ten days, he was dead. When David heard this news, he remembered Abigail and asked her to marry him. She accepted his proposal and became the wife not only of Israel's future king, but of a man after God's own heart.

Abigail, like so many of us, reaped the seeds of a bad choice—her decision to marry Nabal. But the Scriptures constantly teach us that any decision made with a heart toward God—even a bad past decision—will eventually work for the good when placed in God's hands.

From Abigail's story, the tale of a loyal wife married to a drunken fool, I have identified five spiritual truths that will help all of us who are having to live with bad decisions made in the past—whether they were relationship decisions, financial decisions, career decisions, or any other kind.

1. *Trust God's timing.* God is not bound by our clocks and calendars. He is not confined by time. His idea of "perfect timing" is usually much different—and ultimately much better—than ours. So, be patient. Wait on God. All things *will* work together for the good, because we love God and are called according to His purpose.

2. *Don't become bitter in adversity.* Abagail continued to be a faithful and loyal wife, despite being married to a rotten husband. But in the end, God blessed her. God blesses those who stay loyal and kind in trying situations.

3. *Never regret not doing evil.* There are a lot of things we can regret in life. But one thing we should never regret is turning away from the evil we had in mind to do. God always blesses the person who starts to do or say something bad then shows restraint and backs off. God also blesses people who don't hurt other people. Our task is not to straighten other people out; that is the task of the Holy Spirit. Our task is to love others, encourage them, and hold them up to God in prayer.

4) *Persevere when times get tough.* God's Word is filled with good promises. Yes, there will be adversity and tough times; but to experience the blessings and promises of God, we need to press on and hold on. Remember, the kingdom of God runs in cycles, just like the seasons. If we can wait out the winter, as Abigail was willing to do, we will discover that spring has been waiting just around the corner.

5. *Turn all your decisions over to God—past, present, and future.* Ask Him for wisdom to make good decisions, as James 1:5 encourages us: "If any of you lacks wisdom, he should ask God, who gives generously to all without finding fault, and it will be given to him." But know that God can and will work *all things* together. If you love Him and are called according to His purpose, even a bad decision will eventually work for good.

May 1
The Pure Word of God

Your word is a lamp to my feet and a light for my path.
(Psalm 119:105)

Nothing is absolute in this world—nothing, that is, except the Word of God. The Bible is the only thing we know for certain is true. It's the only thing we know, without a doubt, is from God. Everything else is a concept, idea, or imagination from the mind of man. Everything else is something man has dreamed up or thought through using human reasoning.

Mathematical formulas are not absolute and sure. Chemistry formulas are not absolute and sure. Even postulates in the field of physics are not absolute and sure. The only sure thing we have in the world today is the Word of God, the Holy Scriptures.

Yet, there is irony even in that, because the only way the Word of God can be passed from one person to another is through imperfect people.

When you stop and think about it, you might wonder if God made a horrible mistake by giving us the Bible and then telling us to teach it to other people; because the moment we do, we run the Scriptures through our own impure filter, and it is received by others through their impure filters. With dirty filters on both ends, you would think the Word would become polluted along the way.

But God didn't make a mistake. God has purpose, even in this double-filtered process. One is that, as we share His Word with others, it becomes part of us. It is living and active, as Hebrews 4:12 tells us. It gets into us, and that changes us.

Another purpose is that it allows the Holy Spirit, who inspired the Word, to speak to us and through us. When the Spirit is involved, we grow and mature through this process of speaking the Word and hearing it. Over time,

39

lives are touched, our faith is built up, and our impure filters become just a little cleaner day by day.

As you read this right now, the Word is coming out of a dirty filter—me—and entering through a dirty filter—you. You would think it is getting dirty and distorted both going and coming! But the Holy Spirit is able to interpret the pure Word of God to us anyway. Despite our imperfect speaking and hearing, He is able to bring forth perfect truth and life.

Yes, despite our imperfections, God's Word is absolute. It is certain. It is sure. It is alive and active. Regardless of who preaches it or how it is presented, the Holy Spirit will anoint it and use it to draw people to Christ and make us more like Him.

It is impossible for anyone to understand the Bible using human intellect. Paul writes in 1 Corinthians 2:14, "The man without the Spirit does not accept the things that come from the Spirit of God, for they are foolishness to him, and he cannot understand them, because they are spiritually discerned." When we invite the Spirit of God to be our interpreter, however, He opens our eyes to see and our ears to hear the wisdom and truth found on every page.

God did not give us the Bible to hide His wisdom; He gave it to us so we could easily find it. But only through His Spirit will we ever be able to comprehend and apprehend what He has so generously provided to us.

Take every opportunity available to hear good biblical preaching. Read the Bible for yourself; make it an everyday part of your life, and ask the Holy Spirit to teach you as you go.

Trust God's Word. It is the only sure light we have in this dark world.

May 13
Catch the Wave

"Whoever believes in me, as the Scripture has said,
streams of living water will flow from within him."
(John 7:38)

Have you ever wondered how the Holy Spirit works in and through our lives? The Scriptures are clear: The Holy Spirit works through movement. Every time the Holy Spirit is mentioned in the Bible, it is in the context of movement of one sort or another.

Jesus described the Holy Spirit as new wine. New wine is not stagnant or placid; it is ever-expanding and changing. In fact, the process of growing and fermenting new wine is actually quite violent. Place new wine in an old wineskin, the Bible says, and you will have a disaster on your hands. If the new wine of the Holy Spirit is placed in an old, rigid wineskin, the container will burst. No, it must be placed in a new, flexible wineskin that is capable of expanding with it.

You and I must be like new wineskins. We must be flexible and pliable in God's hands, so the Holy Spirit can move and grow in us and through us.

Jesus also described the Holy Spirit as a spring; not a well, which is still water, but a flowing spring of living water—a fast-moving river that flows up out of our innermost being. And as the saying goes, you can never step into the same river twice. When we encounter the Holy Spirit, we should expect things to move, to flow, to change.

Living near the Atlantic Ocean, as I have most of my life, I see the movement of the Holy Spirit like the ocean waves—always ebbing and flowing. At some point a move of the Spirit comes rolling in, splashy and loud; then it moves out, and all is quiet. The wave comes in and washes up high on the shore, then it ebbs and goes back out into the ocean. Soon, though, another wave follows with even more force.

Have you ever noticed that the waves of the ocean seem to work in swells of seven? Each successive wave builds up higher and higher, until the largest wave, the seventh one, crashes in. Then there is a time of quiet—a gentle lapping of seawater on the shore—until the wave energy builds back up, and the process starts all over again.

I believe new waves are building across the church today. It's time to rise up on your surfboards, Church! We've been bobbing in the water long enough. It's time to paddle fast, stand up, and hang ten. The waves of the Holy Spirit are moving beneath us. If we don't get up on our feet and ride them, we may miss them completely. We may miss what God is doing.

In the Book of Acts, we read about all the exciting things that took place in the early church. Over and over again, we read these terms: miracles, signs, and wonders. The New Testament is filled with these terms. Yet, how easy it is for us to put them aside and act as if God is no longer moving! How easy it is to deny the working of the Holy Spirit and let the wave pass beneath us! Instead of taking the risk and rising up on our surfboards, we're content to just float.

There are more waves coming, and they are brimming with miracles, signs, and wonders. This is how the Holy Spirit moves. It is how He moved in Acts 2 on the day of Pentecost, and it is how He moves today.

On Pentecost, the common people responded to the Holy Spirit with awe, wonder, and amazement. The religious leaders, however, were "greatly disturbed."

Don't be so religious that you miss the move of God. Sometimes following God means breaking out of old, religious molds and traditions. It means throwing away the old, rigid wineskins and starting fresh. Do it now. It's time to stand up and ride the wave of God.

May 28
Act Justly, Love Mercy, Walk Humbly

He has showed you, O man, what is good. And what
does the Lord require of you? To act justly and to love
mercy and to walk humbly with your God. (Micah 6:8)

Have you ever wondered what it is that God really
requires from us, His children? Are we working hard
enough to please Him? Are we good enough? Do we
witness enough? Do we give enough? What exactly does
God ask of us as we walk out this Christian experience
with Him?

These questions and others like them have consumed
well intentioned, God-fearing people for centuries. The
simple answer is found in Micah 6:8: "What does the Lord
require of you? To act justly and to love mercy and to
walk humbly with your God."

Micah was an Old Testament prophet who lived
about 700 years before the birth of Christ. He prophesied
God's judgment on Israel and Judah for turning away
from the Lord, as well as their eventual deliverance and
return to Him. Micah's words to God's people about what
God requires were clear and unmistakable, and they are
still valid for us today. In fact, Jesus taught these exact
same principles in His Sermon on the Mount.

What does it mean to act justly? Jesus taught that we
are to do unto others as we would have them do unto us.
That is what "acting justly" means, in a nutshell. We are
to treat people—all people—the way we would want them
to treat us. Acting justly is simply abiding by the Golden
Rule.

What does it mean to love mercy? Mercy can be
defined a number of different ways, but I see mercy as
essentially this: having no agenda to change others—in
other words, loving people the way they are. When we are
merciful, we are genuinely more interested in others than

we are in ourselves. We're more interested in what others think or feel than in what we think or feel.

Let me ask you a few questions. When you are in a conversation with someone, what are you really doing? Are you just waiting for them to stop talking, so you can interject your opinions? Do you leap to conclusions when others confide in you? Or are you genuinely listening to them and interested in what they are saying? Are you hearing their feelings, their fears, their concerns, not just with your ears, but with your heart?

If you are doing the latter, then that is mercy. The other person's thoughts are more important to you than your own opinions. You are not focusing on yourself, demanding to be seen and heard; you are preferring the other person. You are choosing to be generous, compassionate, and forgiving. You're saying, "I want to listen to you, because I want to love you; and I can't love you unless I know you."

Finally, we are told to walk humbly with our God. What does that mean? It means we're to be honest and transparent before Him. When we come to God in prayer, we are to leave all vestiges of pride at the door. We are to speak what is on our hearts openly and truthfully, as children with their loving Father. God hears us when we pray; He hears us when we think and meditate; He even hears us when we dream. That is humbling, especially when we pause to consider that He still loves us and forgives us, despite our imperfections.

So, be honest before God. He already knows everything about you anyway! Allow Him to plant the seeds of justice, mercy, and humility deep in your heart. In time, you will find that a great harvest has grown up within you, and you have been transformed into the kind of man or woman of God that can change the world in His name.

July 30
Walking on Water

"Come," he said. Then Peter got down out of the boat,
walked on the water and came toward Jesus.
(Matthew 14:29)

I believe God's desire is for every believer to rise up to the highest level of greatness possible in this life. It concerns me, however, that so many of us seem to be okay with falling short. We're comfortable where we are. We're satisfied to stay in the middle of the pack, at our current level of mediocrity. It doesn't seem to bother us that, on our current trajectory, we're never going to achieve the dreams, goals, and purposes God has set for us. We're just not willing to do whatever it takes to become the person God wants us to be.

We need a wake-up call! The Holy Spirit didn't come to make us mediocre. He came to challenge us to greatness. He came to give us impossible dreams to pursue and impossible tasks to achieve—and the faith, courage, and power to make the impossible, possible.

All human greatness has its roots in Godlikeness. The Book of Genesis clearly states we have been made in the image of God. That means the Lord has instilled within each of us something of Himself. And if that something is activated through faith in His Son, Jesus, and the infilling of His Holy Spirit, then we have everything we need to do amazing, seemingly impossible things in this life for His glory.

Every person who has ever achieved something "impossible" has been driven by this same God-given, inner incentive to greatness. Think of Christopher Columbus, who sailed across the Atlantic. Or Sir Edmond Hillary, who climbed Mt. Everest. Or Charles Fulton, who built a boat that ran on steam. Or Alexander Graham Bell, who risked everything he had to invent the telephone. Or Peter, who walked on water.

I am inspired by all these men; but I identify with Peter the most. He was not known as a great intellect, a tireless inventor, or a fearless adventurer. He was just a common fisherman. But when Jesus beckoned him in Matthew chapter 14 to leave the safety of the boat and join Him on the waves, he didn't hesitate. He threw his legs over the side. Andrew could have stepped out. John could have. But only Peter did.

Jesus is calling us, as He called Peter, to step out in faith. He is calling each of us to do seemingly impossible things in these latter days. Will it be dangerous? Sure. Will it cost us our lives? That's a distinct possibility. But isn't it better to lose everything than to not attempt the impossible for the glory of God?

God is calling you to walk on water. He is calling you to leave all safety and comfort behind and do something you've never done before. What if you start to sink? That's a risk you will have to take. And that's where faith and trust come in. The strong arm of God is always there to lift you up when you begin to falter.

But it could very well be that, unless God intervenes, you will look like a fool—or a martyr. At least, that is what the world will say. What matters, though, is what God will say: "Well done, good and faithful servant!"

Can you feel that sense of excitement rising up within you? That's the Spirit of God reminding you that you were created to achieve greatness, to live a life of meaning and purpose, even if it costs you everything. So, go ahead; dream big dreams. Pray big prayers. Set that seemingly impossible goal and work toward it with discipline and diligence. Take on that task that is so big, you are bound to fail unless God intervenes. Invest everything you have, including your future, in that great purpose that will give God glory. Step out in faith and do the impossible, because nothing is impossible with God.

August 12
What Can We Expect?

"And afterward, I will pour out my Spirit on all people."
(Joel 2:28)

You and I are living in what the Bible calls the "end times" or the "last days"—that season of history just before Jesus Christ returns to the earth in glory. And according to Scripture, we can expect two things to happen in these last days.

One is described in 2 Thessalonians 2:3: "Don't let anyone deceive you in any way, for that day will not come until the rebellion occurs." Other translations use the term "falling away" instead of "rebellion." As we move toward the end of the age, we can expect a falling away of many people in the church. They will have called themselves Christians; they will have given lip service to Jesus. But when things start to get really tough, they will give up and give in to the pressures of the world. They will "abandon the faith," as 1 Timothy 4:1 says. Unwilling to walk in the power of the Holy Spirit, they will turn their backs on the commission and commands of Christ. They will fall into apostasy.

I realize I'm painting a grim picture. But there is great news, too.

The second thing we can expect in the last days is described in Joel 2:28 and repeated by Peter in Acts 2:17: God will pour out His Holy Spirit on all people. In other words, everyone who desires the Holy Spirit will be filled, and He will come alive in them. That means that as we approach the return of Jesus, we can look forward to a great renewal among those Christians who remain faithful. A Spirit-filled body of believers will emerge in the midst of a dead, apostasy-ridden church.

I'm excited because, as I look around the body of Christ, I see signs that the outpouring has already begun.

I don't know of any Christ-centered church today that doesn't have some sort of evidence of a move of the Holy Spirit, to one degree or another. The promise of the Bible is literally coming to pass. That which was experienced at Pentecost is beginning to be experienced again by God's people all over the world.

Christians everywhere are being filled with the Holy Spirit. As a result, three things are happening: they are receiving the gifts of the Holy Spirit; they're being transformed by the fruit of the Spirit; and they're moving out into the world in the power of the Holy Spirit.

I know that there is a falling away coming. But my prayer is for more and more of the church to be open to the move of God and to experience the power and fulness of the Holy Spirit.

Etched into a cornerstone at the seminary I attended is this command from Jesus found in Matthew 10:7: "As you go, preach"—followed by an ellipsis. An ellipsis is a punctuation mark—dot, dot, dot—that basically means, "there is something more that follows here, but it's not important enough to be included." The truth is, what follows the command to preach is critically important, especially in these last days. If we're going to impact the world for Christ, we will need to do more than preach, as indicated in verse 7. We will need to follow the command in verse 8, too: "Heal the sick, raise the dead, cleanse those who have leprosy, [and] drive out demons."

Church, as we approach the end of the age, we need more than ever to be filled with the Holy Spirit. We can't be the people we've been called to be or do the things Jesus commanded us to do without having the Spirit of God working actively within us. The world needs to see a united, Spirit-filled church.

Listen; do you hear the mighty wind blowing? The Spirit of God is moving. The Holy Spirit is among us. The kingdom of God is at hand.

August 23
When God Speaks

*It was he who gave some to be apostles, some to be
prophets, some to be evangelists, and some to be pastors
and teachers, to prepare God's people for works of
service, so that the body of Christ may be built up.*
(Ephesians 4:11-12)

God wants to speak to us, and He wants to do it
through the church, the body of Christ, as each person
fulfills his or her specific role. The question is, what does
God expect you to do when He sends a message through
an apostle, a prophet, a teacher, a preacher, or an
evangelist?

For one thing, He expects you to hear it and apply it
to your life—not someone else's life. God's message to
you is for *you*. Don't miss hearing God speak into your
life by immediately assuming a message is for your
spouse or your neighbor or the person sitting three rows
in front of you. God is speaking to *you*, and He's speaking
to you on purpose.

In general, when God gives a message through the
church, He wants to do three things:

1. *God wants to reveal Himself.* It is at the very
center of God's heart to reveal Himself to His people. He
is not hiding. We don't have to search far and wide. Islam
and Buddhism and all the other religions of the world are
"seeking" religions. But Christianity is not a religion; it's
a revelation. We don't have to seek anything. All we have
to do is receive what He has already revealed and what He
continues to reveal.

Of course, He has revealed Himself to us, first and
foremost, through His Son, Jesus Christ. But in addition,
God sends other people to us—prophets, teachers, and so
on—to speak messages that pull back the curtain a little
bit more and say, in essence, "Take a look at this. Here is

something God wants you to know about Him. He is revealing Himself to you in this way."

2. *God wants us to receive Him and respond to Him.* God's desire is not only to reveal Himself to us, but also to have us receive Him and respond back to Him in love. He is constantly saying to us, in a thousand different ways, "I love you, I love you, I love you." Our only reasonable response is to love Him in return, as 1 John 4:19 says: "We love because he first loved us."

We show God that we receive Him when we praise Him, worship Him, and tell Him we love Him—not only with our words, but with our lives. We praise Him as we acknowledge that every breath we take is His gift to us. We worship Him as we recognize His creative touch in every flower, every cloud, every snowflake, every face. We receive Him as we accept Jesus Christ as our Savior and God's most perfect and complete revelation, as Jesus Himself said in John 14:9: "Anyone who has seen me has seen the Father."

3. *God wants to reproduce Himself through us.* God wants us to hear and receive and respond to His message, so that we can be filled with His Holy Spirit. It is the mission of the Holy Spirit to reproduce Jesus in us. That way, wherever we go, people will be able to look at us and see Jesus. God wants His Spirit to flow freely through us to others, so that they, too, will receive the revelation of His love for them.

Make it your mission today to hear God when He speaks to you through the body of Christ. Submit yourself to the wisdom and oversight of the apostle. Welcome the prophet when he comes, and listen to him. Respond to the pastor when he puts his arm around you, and receive his encouragement. Pay attention to the teacher as he rightly interprets God's Word. Support the evangelist as he goes out to share that Word with others. Remember, God is speaking to you, and He is speaking to you on purpose. Don't miss it.

August 28
Called, Chosen, Controlled

But you are a chosen people, a royal priesthood, a holy nation, a people belonging to God, that you may declare the praises of him who called you out of darkness into his wonderful light. (1 Peter 2:9)

One day I was out working in the yard, shoveling dirt into a trailer. My three-year-old grandson, TJ, was with me. He wanted to help, but his little shovel, once it was filled with dirt, was too heavy for him to lift. So, he looked up at me standing high in the trailer and said, "Papa, I can't do it. It's too hard for me. Can you do it for me?"

I was overjoyed to help him. He was right—he was too small, and lifting the heavy shovel was too hard. And he was right about something else, too: not only was I strong enough to do it, I was happy to do it, because I loved him.

As TJ and I continued to work together, it occurred to me that this is how God sees us. He has given us a task to do, but because of our weakness, we can't do it. When we finally go to Him and say, "Will you help me, Lord?" He is not only happy to help us; He is thrilled that we asked. He is always ready to help His children. He loves to do the things we ask of Him in His name.

When Jesus came to Earth, He called us out of the darkness of the world and into His marvelous light. The world cannot comprehend the light of Jesus. The Bible says in John 1:5, "The light shines in the darkness, but the darkness has not understood it." But we who have put our faith in Christ have been given grace not only to understand the light, but to walk in it.

Of course, God has been in the business of calling people out of darkness from the very beginning. He has always put His hand on specific individuals and called them by name: Moses, Abraham, Isaac, Jacob, the

51

prophets, the apostles. To this very day, God continues to call people, to choose people.

In fact, the Bible says in 1 Peter 2:9 that you and I, as followers of Jesus, are "a chosen people." The term "chosen" carries with it the idea of being under control. To be chosen by God is to be under the control of God.

We like the idea of being chosen, but controlled? Not so much. Most people don't want someone else to control their lives; they like to be in charge. For unbelievers, that's understandable. They are walking in darkness, and they can't comprehend the light. But we are Christians. We're chosen people, called by Jesus Himself. We are filled with the Holy Spirit. We are no longer walking in darkness; we are walking in the light.

Accepting the call of Christ means making Him Lord. It means giving Him control from that point forward. It means allowing His Holy Spirit to work in us and through us to conform us into His image. We are not in control; Jesus is. As Christians, we have voluntarily put Jesus on the throne of our hearts. He now reigns in us—and "reign" is a word that signifies control.

But please understand: You are not chosen by God so He can have someone to push around. He is not an egomaniac; He is your big, strong, loving heavenly Father. You are chosen by God to be His beloved child who can turn to Him at any time and say, "Papa, it's too heavy for me. Can You do it for me?" His job is to care for you and be in control over the things that concern you. Your job is to "declare the praises of him who called you out of darkness into his wonderful light."

How wonderful it is to be His chosen people! Let's trust the Lord and give Him control over every facet of our lives. Then, let's give Him praise.

September 4
We Are Children of God

Yet to all who received him, to those who believed in his name, he gave the right to become children of God.
(John 1:12)

When God first began to reveal Himself to the ancient world, people considered Him so holy that they wouldn't dare utter His name. He was largely an unknown God to them—a God removed from their daily lives, to be revered at a distance or approached by only the holiest of men. Even the holy men wrote His name without vowels, so it could not be pronounced.

The people believed in God, and they believed they were protected by Him. But it never occurred to them to pursue an intimate relationship with Him. He was God, but He was not a personal God.

Then, at Calvary, everything changed. On the cross, Jesus opened the door between us and God. Now, because of Christ, each of us can know God; and, not just know Him, but also have an intimate, personal relationship with Him. And it goes even further, as John 1:12 confirms: because we have received Jesus into our lives and have believed in His name, we are now declared to be children of God.

And that's not all. Not only does God call us His children, but He has given us the right to call Him by His name. He is God, but He is more than that. He is also our Father. According to Romans 8:15, the Spirit you received brought about your adoption to sonship. And by Him we cry, "*Abba*, Father." In Aramaic, *Abba* is a term of endearment, like "Daddy" or "Papa." Just as I love it when my grandchildren crawl into my lap, God, our heavenly Father, loves it when we crawl into His lap, put our arms around His neck, snuggle close, and call Him "Daddy."

It seems almost too good to be true! We are members of the family of God. We have taken His name. We are blood of His blood. We are not just adopted; we are grafted into His family tree. His name is written on our hearts, and His Spirit indwells us and confirms our unbreakable bond, as Romans 8:16 says: "The Spirit himself testifies with our spirit that we are God's children."

Furthermore, Romans 8:17 tells us "we are heirs of God and co-heirs with Christ." We are not stepchildren. We're not illegitimate. We are fully accepted members of God's family. The inheritance the Father gave to Jesus, He now gives to us, too.

Satan will try to tell you otherwise. Don't listen to him when he whispers, "The inheritance is for others; it's not for you." He will tell you you're not worthy, or you're too sinful, or you're too broken to be accepted by God. But the devil is a liar. We may have been all those things before we met Jesus; but now we are new creations in Christ. He has redeemed us and called us by name. We are righteous in God's sight—not because of anything we do or don't do, but because of what Jesus did.

Today God declares over you, "As a blood-bought follower of My Son, Jesus Christ, you are now My child, too. See? I have set a table of blessing before you. Come, eat, and be filled."

You know, my oldest son, Bruce, used to live in my house. He ate my food. He slept in the bed I bought. He drove the car I paid for. I gave him full access to all these things, because he is my son and my heir, and I love him.

Today God offers you similar access to enter His house and rest and fellowship and partake of every good thing He has prepared for you. Because you are His child and He loves you, He invites you to share in His peace, His joy, His prosperity, and so much more. As an heir of His kingdom, it is all yours. All you have to do is open your heart and receive.

September 25
Good News

"Do not be afraid. I bring you good news of great joy that will be for all the people." (Luke 2:10)

It seems like every time we open the newspaper, we read nothing but bad news. We turn on the TV and see nothing but horrible things happening around the world—and sometimes even next door.

That's why I like to open my Bible before I read the newspaper or turn on the TV. The Bible is full of good news! Why? Because throughout its pages, God speaks. And when God speaks, He has a way of turning bad news into good news.

God spoke to Moses from a burning bush near the base of Mt. Sinai. Before that, the voice of the Lord had not been heard for nearly 500 years. God told him, "I am sending you to Pharaoh to bring My people out of captivity in Egypt." That didn't sound like good news to Moses, since he had been run out of Egypt 40 years earlier with a bounty on his head. But it turned out to be good news for the Israelites he would eventually lead to the Promised Land.

God spoke to Isaiah, saying, "Whom shall I send?" And Isaiah replied, "Send me!" But Isaiah discovered that being God's prophet wasn't necessarily good news. For one thing, much of his message sounded like bad news for the Israelites. When Isaiah complained, God told him, "Don't worry, Isaiah. I am doing so much more in the world than what you see and understand right now." Then He gave Isaiah this word: "The virgin will conceive and give birth to a son, and will call him Immanuel." Isaiah didn't know he was prophesying an event that would take place 700 years later—something that would be good news not only for Israel, but for all mankind.

The angel Gabriel spoke to a teenage girl who was not yet married and told her she was going to have a child. Not only was Mary greatly troubled by the angel's sudden appearance; but being told that she was going to give birth out of wedlock was not good news—especially in a culture where premarital sex was punishable by stoning. But nine months later, Mary gave birth to Jesus, and that is great news for everyone who puts their faith in Him.

Jesus spoke to His disciples not long before His arrest in the garden at Gethsemane. "I will soon be going away," He said. The disciples were sad and confused. This was not the news they wanted to hear. But Jesus said, "It is good for you that I go away, because then I can send the Comforter to you." And He was right. The bad news became good news, not only for those disciples, but for every disciple who believes and receives the Holy Spirit through their testimony.

Jesus spoke from the cross at Calvary, crying out, "It is finished!" Immediately, Satan prepared the next day's headline: "Son of God Crucified, Mankind's Hope Destroyed." But three days later, the worst possible news became the Good News. The death, burial, and resurrection of Jesus was God's plan from the beginning to bring salvation to the whole world—and that includes sinners like you and me.

Are you going through a difficult time right now? Is your health failing? Is your marriage crumbling? Are you struggling to keep your head above water? If you were to write a headline over your life today, would it be bad news?

Take heart! God is a master at taking bad news and transforming it. Whatever you're experiencing right now, it is not the end of the story. God's plan for your life is good, and it goes far beyond what you see and understand at this moment. Jesus Christ *is* the Good News. Give Him your life, and He will write a new headline for you.

December 31
The Land That Has No Paths

My times are in your hands; deliver me from my enemies and from those who pursue me. (Psalm 31:15)

When I was going through a particularly difficult time in my life, I called my 90-year-old mother and asked her to pray for me. After I explained what was going on, I told her I had determined to no longer trust in my own abilities and intellect. "From now on," I said, "I am committed to seeking God at every intersection."

Her reply stunned me. "No, son, you can't do that," she said, "because you are walking in a land that has no paths. There are no intersections because, where you're going, there are no trails. Instead, you must seek God at every step. Don't wait to reach a crossroads before you cry out to Him. Don't wait for a decision point. Seek the Lord with every step you take, each minute of every day."

Suddenly, I realized that is exactly what God had always wanted me to do. For too long, I had been doing things in my own wisdom and strength. I had been plodding along through life, thinking that because a certain way seemed right to me, it must be God's way.

But God wants me—He wants us—to seek Him at every step. He wants us to live each day as if it is our last. Of course, we stand in faith, believing we have many more days to come; but as David said in Psalm 31:14-15, "I trust in you, Lord . . . my times are in your hands."

I'm reminded of an ancient nautical chart I saw, similar to one Christopher Columbus would have used. For navigating along the coast, the chart no doubt provided a lot of useful information to sailors in that day. But beyond a certain point out to sea, the chart maker could only use his imagination; so he scrawled, "Beyond this, there be dragons!"

How do you sail uncharted seas? How do you walk where there is no path? You do it with your hand in God's hand and His word in your heart. There *are* dragons out there, but they cannot harm a child of God. They cannot take you, because they have no right to you. God has already spoken for you. You are His. You are under His full protection.

There is no map or chart to lead us through this life except the Bible, God's Word to us. It is the only written guide we have to go by. In addition, God has promised to personally direct our steps as we walk with Him across this land that has no paths. He will guide us with His voice, as Isaiah 30:21 says: "Whether you turn to the right or to the left, your ears will hear a voice behind you, saying, 'This is the way; walk in it.'" We simply have to tune out all the other non-essential noises and listen for the whisper of God.

We must listen, because the way is not without peril. Our enemy, Satan, has scattered mines throughout the land. They are set to explode if we take one false step. But as long as we listen for God's voice and walk with Him step by step, we have nothing to fear; He will lead us safely through every minefield.

You know, we can choose to live each day as if it is the last day of our lives, or we can choose to live each day as if it is the first. Both perspectives have value. But whichever we choose, let's determine to live each day fully engaged with the God of life. He loves us, and He wants to lead us, bless us, and empower us through His Word, by His voice, and with His very presence.

So, put your hand in His. Listen for His voice; and when you hear Him, obey. Go the way He directs. Don't try to run ahead, thinking you know the way. Instead, seek Him for each step, and take one step at a time. Remember, you are walking through a land that has no paths. But your heavenly Father knows where He wants you to go, and He knows the way to get you there.

Available Books by Jamie Buckingham

Risky Living
A Way Through the Wilderness
Where Eagles Soar
Coping with Criticism
The Nazarene (a 50-day devotional)
Jesus World (a novel)
The Truth Will Set You Free . . .
. . . But First it Will Make You Miserable
Bible People Like Me
*Miracles of Jesus (*a.k.a. *Miracle Power)*
Parables of Jesus
Into the Glory
Some Gall
The Last Word
Spiritual Maturity
A Spirit-Led Life (testimonial sermon series by Jamie)
The Brightness of Your Rising (sermon series by Jamie)
Thoughts from the Heart of God(compiled Jamie quotes)
Armed for Spiritual Warfare
Power for Living
Pits Along the Road to Glory

Booklets from Teachings by Jamie Buckingham

*God is in Control; When Your Prayers Go Unanswered;
Senior Saints; Laughing at Life; Unproductive Seasons;
When You Are Born Ugly; Essentials for Hearing God;
How to Get Ready to Die; Activating Angels through
Prayer; Healing for Today; Perseverance and God's
Faithfulness; The Weights of Life; Thanksgiving in the
Pit; How to Raise the Dead; Inside the Kingdom of God;
The Nature of God; Shaken by God; Shadow Ministry;
They Left Their Nets; Victory Over Discouragement;
The Lordship of Jesus; Who is God?*

For more information about Jamie Buckingham
and his ministry, please visit
www.JamieBuckinghamMinistries.com.
His books, columns, additional writings, video
devotional series, and audio and video sermons can
be found on this website, which is dedicated to
preserving his life works.

Risky Living Ministries, Inc.

www.RLMin.com

ORDER FORM: MEETING GOD DEVOTIONAL

Name _____

Address _____

City _____ State _____ Zip _____

Email address _____

1 book @ $27.00   *   2-4 books @ $25.00 per book **5 or more books @ $23.00 per book**

Number desired _____ Amount enclosed $_____

(U.S. mainland shipping included!)

Make checks payable to Risky Living Ministries, Inc.

<u>For Credit Card purchases</u>

Date _____ Total amount charged $_____

Name on Card _____

☐ **VISA** ☐ **Mastercard** ☐ **AMEX**

Account#_____

Expiration Date ___/___/_____ CVV/CVD _____

Billing Zip Code _____

Mail to: **Risky Living Ministries, Inc.**
3901 Hield Road, NW
Palm Bay, FL 32907

ORDER FORM: MEETING GOD DEVOTIONAL

Name _____

Address _____

City _____State _____ Zip _____

Email address _____

> **1 book @ $27.00 * 2-4 books @ $25.00 per book**
> **5 or more books @ $23.00 per book**

Number desired _____ Amount enclosed $_____
(U.S. mainland shipping included!)

Make checks payable to Risky Living Ministries, Inc.

For Credit Card purchases

Date _____ Total amount charged $_____

Name on Card _____

☐ **VISA** ☐ **Mastercard** ☐ **AMEX**

Account#_____

Expiration Date ___/___/____ CVV/CVD _____

Billing Zip Code _____

Mail to: **Risky Living Ministries, Inc.**
          3901 Hield Road, NW
          Palm Bay, FL 32907

ORDER FORM: MEETING GOD DEVOTIONAL

Name _____

Address _____

City _____ State _____ Zip _____

Email address _____

| 1 book @ $27.00 * 2-4 books @ $25.00 per book |
| 5 or more books @ $23.00 per book |

Number desired _____ Amount enclosed $_____
(U.S. mainland shipping included!)

Make checks payable to Risky Living Ministries, Inc.

For Credit Card purchases

Date _____ Total amount charged $_____

Name on Card _____

☐ **VISA** ☐ **Mastercard** ☐ **AMEX**

Account#_____

Expiration Date ___/___/____ CVV/CVD _____

Billing Zip Code _____

Mail to: **Risky Living Ministries, Inc.**
3901 Hield Road, NW
Palm Bay, FL 32907

Made in the USA
Columbia, SC
06 February 2023

11197946R00037